The Most Beautiful Cats

The Most Beautiful Cats

Claude Pacheteau

Photographs by Agence Horizon

Flammarion

Contents

Above: Russian Blue kittens
Facing page: Chausie, brown ticked tabby

Preface

All kittens are adorable bundles of fur. Yet, in the space of a few weeks, as they grow, they will be completely transformed. But their development is not only physical; great differences in character and temperament are also observed among the various breeds of cat.

By selecting a good breeder who socializes his kittens correctly, the future owner can be more sure of what his cat will be like in adulthood. He or she will thereby avoid disappointment and unpleasant surprises.

This second volume introduces a number of breeds, from the best known to the most rare, to help you discover them, be more discerning in your choice, or let you learn more about your four-legged friend.

You might be looking for a loveable, purring tomcat or perhaps an independent feline? Or is your lifestyle better suited to spending time with a teasing, dynamic cat? Each entry describes the characteristic features of the personality of the breed in question, as well as the key points of the breed's physical appearance, insofar as they correspond to the standards in force. Information is also given on the strengths and weaknesses in terms of health, grooming, and education. And these entries also provide you with the full range of names given to each breed, its country of origin, its ancestors, and the history of the breed's creation.

Right: young Maine Coon, cream blotched tabby and white
Facing page: Siberian, Neva Masquerade blue tabby

ABYSSINIAN

Other names: rabbit cat, bunny cat, hare cat, British Tick, Aby
Country of origin: Ethiopia (formerly called Abyssinia)
Ancestors: African wildcat (*Felis silvestris lybica*)
Coat: springy to the touch ("resilient"), lustrous sheen, short, and fine
Colors: 28 colors authorized in total: ruddy, blue, sorrel (cinnamon), fawn, chocolate, lilac, tawny, cream, tortie (tortoiseshell), silver. Ticked tabby remains the classic pattern.

Described in its standard as having a "regal appearance," the Abyssinian has a muscular, medium-sized body type. Males are larger than females. Its coat is "ticked" but, being light reflective, has a unified appearance. "Ticking," a characteristic of the breed, refers to the presence of alternating light and dark bands on each hair shaft, with the exception of the underside, neck, chest, and the insides of the legs, which are unticked. The coat is darker at the spine, and the original ruddy color remains the most popular. The Abyssinian's distinctive coat gives it the delightful effect of a small wildcat. Indeed, it is this "wild" streak that has made it such a success.

The head has rounded contours without flat planes. Large and almond-shaped, the eyes are expressive, uniform in color, and range from yellow to hazel. The ears are large and cupped forward, with a typical "thumbprint" marking on the outer side.

The Abyssinian is one of the oldest breeds of cat. It was allegedly created or enhanced in Great Britain as early as the nineteenth century, using a cat brought back from Ethiopia. The Abyssinian soon caught US interest, where the breed enjoys great success.

Elegant and harmonious, Abyssinians are lithe and nimble. Being playful and very active, they use their physical agility fully in their daily behavior. Curious and bold, they become less impetuous with age but

Abyssinian, sorrel

Abyssinian, ruddy

remain very playful. Sufficient space and, if possible, a garden are therefore recommended to enable them to give vent to their vitality.

Exceedingly loyal, they become highly attached to their masters and demand constant attention. This deep attachment means that they can at times be somewhat clingy. This unbounded affection is offset by the fact that they hate solitude and need to be fully involved in family life.

Breeders emphasize the intelligence of these cats that are quick on the uptake—a character trait that makes their education easier.

Their short, silky fur requires only the limited maintenance of a weekly brushing. Healthwise, the breed is prone to a genetic disease, amyloidosis, which takes the form of progressive renal insufficiency, though this fortunately remains rare.

AMERICAN CURL

Country of origin: United States (California)
Ancestors: domestic cat
Coat: two varieties: shorthair (short and silky with little undercoat), or longhair (medium length, fine, and silky, minimal undercoat)
Colors: all

The American Curl owes its name to its ears, which are curled back in a regular arc. They are firm at the base and flexible at the tips. Various degrees of curvature are possible as the curl gene—though dominant—is of variable expression. Some cats therefore present very slight curl and others more; crescent-shaped ears remain the most highly prized form. Two varieties are possible: shorthair and longhair. This breed, which developed in the early 1980s in the United States, remains very rare, particularly outside of America.

The American Curl owes the highly distinctive form of its ears—the main feature of the breed—to a genetic mutation that arose spontaneously on a black stray cat, Shulamith, adopted by a Californian family in 1981. Selective breeding on the initiative of a family friend who was a breeder began with this cat and its descendants in 1983. Selection confirmed the dominance of the mutated gene at the origin of the curling ears. The breed remains fairly undeveloped today.

The American Curl is a cat of intermediate body type (known as "semi-foreign"). Curled-back ears distinguish the medium-sized head, slightly longer than it is wide and with virtually no break. The standard refuses excessive curvature (the tip of the ear touching the back of the ear for instance); the same goes

American Curl Longhair, red tabby point

for the other extreme of straight ears or those with asymmetrical curls. The eyes, preferably brilliant and brightly colored, are walnut-shaped. Bone structure is medium-sized, and musculature is well developed. The tail is flexible and is as long as the body.

Unions of two American Curls pose no particular problems and are permitted. However, as the American Curl population is still very limited in number, it is advisable to alternate crossbreeding with cats with normal ears to avoid risks of inbreeding. The ears begin to take on a curled form around the age of one week but do not acquire their definitive form until around four months.

The Curl, as it is nicknamed, is a cat with a balanced nature, both playful and smart, while at the same time being easy and pleasant to live with. They are not mute, but seldom let you hear the sound of their voice.

Sociable and affectionate, they become very attached to their masters and generally have no problems in accepting their own kind, as well as their fellow inhabitants of all shapes and sizes. Friendly with children, they are active and affectionate, and require space for their daily exercise. They are therefore better suited to a house with garden than to being confined to an apartment.

Maintenance poses no problems for either the longhair or shorthair division, as a weekly brushing suffices. The ears should be cleaned with a suitable veterinary product.

American Curl Longhair, blue cream tabby point

TURKISH ANGORA

Country of origin: Turkey
Ancestors: very ancient breed, originating from cats present in the Turkish capital, now Ankara, which was formerly known as Angora
Coat: medium length, fine and silky, with little undercoat. The fur is longest at the ruff, the britches, the underbelly, and on the tail.
Colors: white is the most highly prized, but other colors are recognized

Elegance is the first word that springs to mind when looking at a Turkish Angora. With their fine, silky coats, they are very graceful. Yet this apparent daintiness hides a "dense," muscular cat. This breed is probably one of the most ancient in the world. The Turkish Angora was the first longhaired cat to arrive in Europe in the sixteenth century. Siring the Persian in the 1900s, the breed remains quite uncommon and has become somewhat outshone by its Persian offspring. In Turkey, this purebred, which almost disappeared, is today protected.

Native to Ankara, whose former name it adopted, the Turkish Angora is one of the world's oldest cats, and myths and legends punctuate its history. It was highly appreciated by the aristocracy of France, notably at the court of Louis XV, and even of Europe. The breed almost became extinct after World War II and owes its salvation to the work of passionate breeders in Europe and the US, who imported specimens from Turkey and set about redressing the numbers, while retaining their original purity.

The term "angora" has today become commonplace, used to refer to any longhaired cat—much to the displeasure of the breed's purists! Graceful cats, of medium type (known as "foreign"), their heads are relatively small for the long, fine, and muscular bodies.

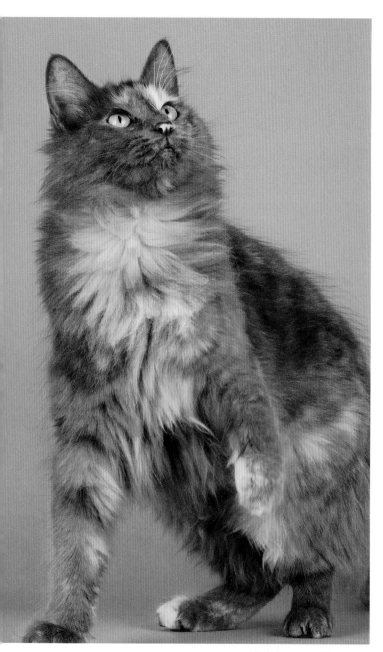

Turkish Angora, blue cream

Turkish Angora, blue cream

They are delicate in appearance only, being in reality robust and athletic. Furthermore, they are great hunters and require space. The Turkish Angora is a concentrate of all the assets of feline seduction: silky, gossamer fur, natural elegance, long slim legs, and a long bushy tail.

The ears are large and set high on the head with, if possible, a tuft of hair on the tips, giving the cat a wild look. The big almond-shaped eyes vary in color depending on the coat, but bright blue is desirable.

The Angora is a cat that is easy to live with, affectionate, and playful. According to fanciers, their education is easy and they learn quickly. A Turkish Agora on a leash is not an uncommon sight! Behind their active and playful façade, they are sensitive souls who are very close to their masters and look for signs of affection. Though quite vocal, their light mewing makes them discreet. Sociable and adaptable, they are at ease anywhere and get on well with dogs and cats if accustomed to them at an early age.

The virtual absence of undercoat makes maintenance easy; a weekly brushing suffices.

Balinese, cinnamon tabby point

BALINESE

Other names: Longhair Siamese
Country of origin: United States
Ancestors: Siamese
Coat: medium length, fine and silky, with slight undercoat
Colors: identical to those of the Siamese. In the United States, cats of colors other than seal, blue, chocolate, and lilac point are called Javanese.

The Balinese has all the characteristics of the Siamese, with medium-length hair to boot. Svelte and rangy, it has a long, triangular head (or wedge), straight in profile. The hair is longer on the stomach, the body, and the tail. There is a marked contrast between the color of the points and the coat's ground. As in the Siamese, kittens are born white and do not attain their definitive color until the age of one year.

The origins of the Balinese remain quite hazy. Though undeniably a descendant of the Siamese, it is impossible to state with certainty whether the emergence of the medium-length hair variety is due to a spontaneous mutation or to older crosses, particularly with Persians, belatedly rendered in the appearance of longhaired kittens in Siamese litters.

In any event, longhaired kittens were regularly found among Siamese litters. Initially disparaged and considered worthless, these kittens finally gained in esteem at the end of World War II. A Californian specialist even began to raise these longhaired Siamese specifically. The first subjects were shown in 1955, and the breed was first recognized in the United States in 1970. Other countries followed suit.

The Balinese shares a similar standard to those of the Siamese, Oriental, and Mandarin, differing only in the sections dealing with the coat (in its length and colors) and eye color. They have the same intense blue eye color as the Siamese. Unions with Siamese, Mandarins, and Orientals are permitted.

In terms of character, the Balinese is very much like the Siamese—just as lively and extroverted. Yet their mewing is slightly less brutal and their character more moderate and less exclusive. Playful and curious, they constantly demand their owners' attention, seeking to be stroked and caressed. Sensitive souls, at times they cling to their masters like glue.

These sentimentalists adore company and hate solitude. They come across as being rather sociable and are even generally attracted to their own kind and other household pets.

Skillful hunters, they will be overjoyed to have the use of a garden or a space to work off surplus energy, but they can also live in an apartment as long as they receive enough attention and toys to stave off boredom. The most important way to guarantee their well-being is to involve them fully in family life.

They do not molt heavily and their medium-length hair does not tend to tangle. Careful brushing is therefore sufficient to maintain their fur.

Balinese, blue tabby point

Bengal, tabby seal point

BENGAL

Other names: Bengali, Bengal cat
Country of origin: United States
Ancestors: Asian leopard cat, *Felis bengalensis*
Coat: short and fine, plentiful and soft to the touch
Colors: spotted (markings of various colors on an orange-colored ground) or marble (marbled patterns on the flanks and shoulders). The stomach inevitably carries markings.

The wild origins of this cat are proven, but they have been tempered with selections that have given rise to a true pet. The Bengal has nonetheless retained its little wildcat look that is so popular. They have also kept their wild ancestors' immoderate taste for water, which is far from the case in the majority of the cat family.

Two coat patterns are accepted: spotted and marble. The spotted motif may take two forms: rosettes (preferably) or spots. In the marble pattern, the motifs are scattered randomly but are more concentrated in the center.

This little apartment wildcat was born in the United States in the 1960s, on the initiative of Jean Mill and her work on cat hybridization. The Bengal emerged by a chance encounter in 1963, in the crossing of a female Asian leopard cat (*Felis bengalensis*) and a domestic cat. The second stage in the selection followed in the 1980s and was the subject of a specific program that led to the current breed.

Today, the Bengal is to be found in various countries. The breed is now well established and hybridizations with *Felis bengalensis*, though still performed, are no longer necessary. The Bengal is a fairly large cat, with a long and powerful body, endowed with a strong bone structure.

As wildness is etched into this cat's genes, breeding conditions are of the utmost importance; breeders

Bengal, brown marble tabby

center their selection and rearing activities around kitten socialization in order to erase any residual wild aspects that are still potentially present. For a maximum guarantee of the cat's character and its stability, most federations do not accept individuals for show earlier than fourth generation (F4).

Selection has led to cats that are balanced and pleasant to live with, attentive and curious. They are very active, as is borne out by their muscular bodies; they are curious, but at times a little exclusive in their relationships with their masters. Behind the athletic appearance, the Bengal is a playful but loving cat that has retained a highly developed hunting instinct and therefore needs space.

Now a perfect family cat, the Bengal dislikes solitude; if they are to be left alone, it is preferable to offer them the company of another cat. Selection has considerably softened the Bengal's character and they should be neither timorous nor aggressive.

Regular brushing is sufficient for the maintenance of the short hair.

RUSSIAN BLUE

Other names: Russian, Russian shorthair, Archangel blue, Blue foreign, Maltese
Country of origin: Russia
Ancestors: blue cats from the port of Arkhangelsk (Archangel), on the White Sea
Coat: short, dense, very fine, silky, with a very dense undercoat. The hair is similar to an otter's.
Colors: even blue-gray with silvery sheen. The shades of blue range from light blue (the most highly prized) to dark blue. A black variety and a white one have been developed but are not recognized by the majority of feline associations.

With its slender body and typical blue-gray coloring that is light reflective giving it a silvery sheen, the Russian Blue is a fine, elegant cat, cutting a very aristocratic figure. The large eyes are bright green, with the definitive color being reached only after a year. Ghost tabby markings that disappear around the age of one may be present on kittens. Prolonged exposure to the sun may give the coat a reddish tinge. Besides its color, the fur is marked by its soft texture and plushness, enhanced by the presence of a thick undercoat.

The origins of the Russian Blue are controversial. According to the most commonly held hypothesis, its ancestors hail from the Archangel Isles in Russia, where blue cats make popular pets but are also hunted for their fur. In the late nineteenth century, British sailors brought back a few specimens. Enchanted by them, an English breeder, Mrs. Caraw-Cox, began importations in 1890, undertaking a breeding program using these Russian cats.

The cat was officially named Russian Blue in 1939. After World War II, breeders set about saving the virtually decimated breed, resorting to outcrossings with other breeds (such as British blue and Siamese).

Breeding developed at the same time in the United States, the nation that boasts the largest Russian Blue population today. The Russian Blues there tend to be lighter with paler fur. Since the 1960s, European breeders have endeavored to regain the breed's archetype, from which they digressed through outcrossings with other breeds.

Often confused with the Chartreux, Russian Blues are distinguished by their finer appearance, green eyes, and angular head with seven planes. The slightly upcurled corners of their mouths give them a naturally smiling expression.

This dainty cat likes peace and quiet and hates agitation. Lively and athletic, they are fearsome hunters. Independent and with a dominant streak, they do not take kindly to restraints. Their education should take this into account, and brusqueness is inadvisable. Sensitive souls, they are affectionate with their masters but highly reserved toward strangers.

Maintenance is easy, with weekly brushing and polishing being sufficient.

BOMBAY

Country of origin: United States (Kentucky)
Ancestors: Burmese and American Shorthair
Coat: short, fine, very close-lying with satin-like texture.
It is compared to patent lambskin.
Colors: jet-black only

With its jet-black, deep, gleaming coat with a satin feel and its coppery eyes, the Bombay has an unmistakable look all its own. Its physique is not unlike that of a black panther and its name was, for that matter, chosen in reference to the black leopard of India. Recognized in the late 1970s, the breed remains rare and is seldom found in Europe but enjoys great success in the United States.

A pure product of selection, the Bombay owes itself to an American breeder, Nikki Horner who, in her quest to obtain the black Burmese of her dreams, crossed a Sable Burmese female with a black American Shorthair with copper-colored eyes. This outcrossing, subsequently fine-tuned through a methodical program of selection, gave rise to the Bombay, which is very much a miniature black panther.

Despite its unusual physique, the breed has a hard time developing outside the US where it originated. Yet it compels a clear fascination from the public, as is apparent from the shows where it is exhibited.

Heavier than its size and appearance would have us believe, the Bombay is a stocky cat, cobby in format—a term adopted with reference to its compact body and well-developed rib cage. It has a solid bone structure and musculature. The head is rounded and the muzzle relatively short. The large, round eyes range from copper to gold, though copper remains the preference. Their color is not definitively fixed until around the age of six months. Like the coat, the skin and pads are also black.

No white markings should stand out against the black of the coat. Unions with representatives from the two breeds at the origin of its creation—the Sable Burmese and the black American Shorthair—are permitted.

Gay, lively, and rather extroverted, Bombays make for merry companions, always ready to play. Curious and sure of themselves, they are afraid of nothing. And this boldness is put to good use in one of their favorite activities: hunting. Their performance is all the more remarkable given their surprising agility. Paradoxically, they are also able to curb this exuberance and appear very gentle and calm in the household and with their masters.

Highly sociable, they adapt easily and accept other animals around them, if accustomed to do so. Affectionate and loving with their masters, they sometimes appear exclusive in their relationships and somewhat possessive. As a result, they do not take kindly to solitude. They are vocal, but less so than their ancestor the Burmese.

The short hair makes for very easy grooming.

British Shorthair, lilac

BRITISH SHORTHAIR

Other name: British
Country of origin: Great Britain
Ancestors: common English domestic cat
Coat: short, dense, firm, well bodied
Colors: all. However, white markings are only accepted in parti-color cats.

The British Shorthair is a well-rounded cat. Medium to large in size, it is robust and teddy bear–like, an effect reinforced by the round head, full cheeks, and large round eyes. The fur is very dense, with a thick undercoat. The original blue color remains the most widespread. Its "cobby" format refers to its short, sturdy body type with its heavy bone structure and round head. It exudes a soft, good-natured appearance in keeping with its character.

The British Shorthair, the British equivalent of the European Shorthair, has been around for centuries in the UK but was not recognized until the late nineteenth century, beginning with the cat show at London's Crystal Palace in 1871. Selections only really got underway a few years later, and the breed soon became very popular in Great Britain. Unfortunately, the arrival of foreign breeds of cats, considered less commonplace by viewers, outshone it somewhat and, at the end of World War II, numbers had reached their lowest levels ever. Breeders had to resort to outcrossings with Persian cats to redress the balance, which also gave rise to the medium-length variety, the British Longhair. The situation was then reversed, with the British being used as foundation stock in various programs for other races.

Today the British is to be found throughout the world and has the success it deserves. Its well-rounded appearance, wide range of colors, and pleasant, easygoing nature are key assets.

In addition to their appealing and reassuring "teddy-bear look," these cats have a wonderful character. A friend of all the family, they are not exclusive in their affection but are very attached to their masters. Affectionate and even loving, they are also sociable with their own kind. Yet they know how to make themselves respected!

The placid exterior conceals a curious, playful cat that is not very vocal but very much a part of things. They have an even, balanced nature, which makes them very easy to live with. Adaptable to any situation, with the right degree of attention they are at ease anywhere, town and countryside alike. Despite their lumpish air, they retain their aptitude for hunting. Yet, for all that, they do not denigrate creature comforts and do appreciate a comfy sofa.

Maintenance is easy, as a weekly brushing suffices. Nevertheless, brushing should be more frequent during molting periods, which can be spectacular.

British Shorthair, chocolate

BURMESE

Country of origin: Burma
Ancestor: brown cats called Rajahs
Coat: very short, fine, silky and glossy, very soft to the touch
Colors: four basic varieties: sable (dark brown), blue, chocolate, lilac (pale gray), to which are added new colors, not recognized in the United States: red, cream, and tortie varieties

The Burmese is distinguished by its characteristic coat, with the color being more pronounced at the extremities and on the back, giving the impression of a face mask and marking the paws and tail. This distinctive coat pattern is known as "sepia." No white markings are acceptable. At birth, kittens do not have their definitive colors, which only become established around two and a half months. Likewise, their eyes change from an initial gray-blue to golden yellow.

Initially considered as varieties, the American and British types were established as two distinct breeds in 2004. The American Burmese is a fairly compact, stocky cat, with a round head, a short round muzzle, and a well-defined break, while the British or European Burmese is more slender, with a triangular wedge, prominent cheekbones, and a strong chin.

In the sixteenth century the ancestors of the Burmese—"Rajah" cats—lived in Buddhist temples in what was then Burma. They were brought to England, where they were called "Chocolate Siamese." Known in Europe from the late nineteenth century, the breed fell into slow decline due to its lack of popularity. It owes its salvation to the work of Dr. Joseph Thompson, in the United States. In 1930 he imported from Burma the first

American Burmese, sable

specimen, a female called Wong Mau, who is considered the mother of today's Burmese. The breed is now divided into two—the American and British (or European) types—with morphological differences appearing during the selections carried out on the two continents.

Despite their medium build, Burmese are very muscular and athletic, giving an impression of strength and power in a small package. With their gold eyes and short, silky hair, particularly soft to the touch, they are refined and elegant.

This sophisticated beauty is not the Burmese's sole asset, as it also boasts a wonderful character, common to both the American and European types.

Quite vocal, Burmese are affectionate, sociable cats who enjoy the company of humans and of their own kind and other animals. Extroverts with a strong personality, they are daring cats, afraid of nothing. Cheerful and playful, they are fairly boisterous when young but mellow with age.

Nicknamed "dog-cats" by the breed's connoisseurs, they need to be fully involved in family life and suffer if left out of things. Tending to cling to their masters, they are also very sociable with visitors.

Grooming is easy and limited to a weekly brushing.

English Burmese, lilac

CHARTREUX

Other name: Chartreux cat
Country of origin: France
Coat: dense, of short to medium length, woolly texture, with a plush undercoat
Colors: all shades of even gray-blue

This robust, shorthaired cat is distinguished by its uniform blue-gray color. All shades are acceptable, but preference goes to lighter colors. The fur's impression of thickness and density is accentuated by the presence of a plush undercoat. The cheeks are very full, particularly in males. The round eyes can range from yellow to orange.

The jewel of French cat rearing, the Chartreux is a very old breed whose origins remain hazy. Its ancestors may hail from the Middle East, being introduced into France during the Crusades. Its presence in France is attested by the writings of Du Bellay, Buffon, and Linné, all of whom refer to cats with blue coats. The origins of this cat's name is controversial; some associate it with a type of wool known as "Chartreux pile" in reference to the distinctive texture of its thick coat.

In any event, the Chartreux began to win renown in French breeding circles in the late 1920s, on the initiative of the Léger sisters. They exhibited their first subjects from 1931 onward, and an initial standard was drawn up in 1939. The breed's purity narrowly missed being jeopardized in the 1960s, when breeders made frequent outcrossings with blue British Shorthairs. The relentless efforts of passionate breeders who endeavored to differentiate the two breeds paid off and the Chartreux regained its status of national breed in 1977. Widespread in France, the breed is still not recognized in Great Britain, where it continues to be confused with the British Shorthair.

Of medium build, with a muscular and robust body, the Chartreux is a graceful cat, characterized by its uniform blue-gray color, woolly fur, and incomparable eyes. Its star's physique, combined with a pleasant character, has propelled it to the top ranks of France's favorite felines.

Highly sociable, the Chartreux paradoxically retains a certain element of independence. Very much involved in the household, they are often nicknamed "dog-cats" as they hate to be overlooked! Cats of few words, they are partial to tender loving care and affection. Intelligent and good-natured, they adapt to both apartment and countryside living, where their hunting talents will be put to good use. Balanced and rustic, the Chartreux is a robust cat, quiet and independent, as well as being playful and affectionate—in short, easy to live with!

The thick fur requires regular currying, slightly more often during spring and fall molting periods. A sedentary way of life, combined with a healthy appetite, means that a degree of vigilance is needed as to the contents of their bowls to avoid any risk of obesity.

CHAUSIE

Country of origin: United States/Egypt
Ancestors: *Felis chaus* (Jungle Cat), domestic cat
Coat: short, lying close to the body, with a silky,
supple undercoat
Colors: three recognized colors: black, brown ticked tabby,
and black silver tipped, a color specific to the breed.
Ticking (alternating light and dark bands on each hair shaft)
is characteristic of brown ticked tabbies and silver tipped.
No white lockets are acceptable.

A large cat with a wild bearing and typical gait, the Chausie's distinguishing features include the tufts on the tips of the tall, wide ears; a thick tail shorter than that of domestic cats (measuring around three-quarters of normal length); and a triangular and angular head. The eyes are gold, yellow, hazel, or light green in color. The body is long and substantial, with strong musculature. The feet are small and rounded.

A hybrid of the Chaus cat (*Felis chaus*), a small wildcat weighing in at some 33 pounds (15 kilograms) and found mainly in Egypt but also as far away as Southeast Asia, the Chausie was born in the United States in the 1970s.

As in other breeds of cat with a "wild" phenotype, the aim was to create a cat with a similar physique to that of it wild ancestor, coupled with the character of a domestic cat. The first hybridizations were performed between *Felis chaus* and pedigree domestic cats (Abyssinians, Orientals, and Bengals) or those with no pedigree but with a wild appearance.

The breed is still in its infancy and selection work is underway to determine its characteristics. Outcrossings with Abyssinians and nonpedigree domestic cats are

Chausie, brown ticked tabby

permitted but remain a controversial matter as some breeders claim that this leads to reductions in the Chausie size. First-generation male Chausie cats are sterile, as are the majority of F2 males.

With its wild look, lynx ears, and short tail, the Chausie cuts a distinctive figure. Yet the wildness is in physique only as, character-wise, they are gentle and very playful cats. For that matter, it is a good idea to prepare several toys to keep them busy!

Highly active, intelligent, and curious, they are forever exploring new places or trying out new games. Couch potatoes should abstain from owning them— the Chausie needs action!

Given its origins, this cat needs to be fully socialized when very young. If this stage is carried out carefully, the Chausie will be a pleasant cat to live with, loyal and affectionate, fearless yet not aggressive. Their natural suppleness and agility make them remarkable hunters.

Graceful and elegant, built for hunting, speed, and leaping, this unusual cat, officially recognized as a new breed by TICA since 2003, is still virtually unknown outside of the United States.

The Chausie is a sturdy creature. Given the nature of its coat, maintenance consists of a good, regular brushing to eliminate loose hairs and dirt.

Chausie, brown tabby

Cornish Rex, black smoke and white

CORNISH REX

Other name: Rex
Country of origin: Great Britain
Ancestors: British alley cats and other breeds, namely the Siamese
Coat: short, very soft to the touch, notched, forming washboard waves reminiscent of astrakhan
Colors: all

The Cornish Rex is distinguished by its notched coat, which typically gives it a crimped appearance. The large ears set high on the head add to this original look. The svelte, muscular body and arched back contribute to its elegant, purebred bearing, leading to comparisons with the greyhound. Standing high on its legs, it has the finest bone structure of the entire feline race.

The crimped aspect of the coat is due to a recessive type of mutation, and much inbreeding was therefore required to create the breed.

The Cornish Rex first appeared in England, in the region of Cornwall in 1950—a curly-haired male named Kallibunker was one of the litter born to a tricolor barn cat. The owner, Mrs. Ennismore, who happened to breed rabbits, compared it to a variety of curly-haired lagomorpha, the Rex or Astra rabbit, whose fur was similar to that of the astrakhan lamb. The cat's name was therefore self-evident. To establish the coat characteristic, breeders set about tracking down and crossing curly-haired feline individuals, the mutation being recessive in type. A high degree of inbreeding, combined with outcrossings with other breeds—notably the Siamese and Burmese—led to the breed's creation and its recognition, first in England in 1967, and then progressively by all cat clubs.

The first Cornish Rex pair was introduced in France in 1960 from Germany. The breed arrived in the United States around the same time, and a breeding program got underway. Owing to outcrossings with Siamese and Orientals, American specimens are finer and more nimble than their heavier English counterparts with a more triangular wedge.

As a general rule, the head is longer than it is wide, without going as far as the extreme Oriental type. The chin is relatively firm. The hair is shorter on the head and legs and is more like downy velvet. Overall, the Cornish Rex presents a rangy, convex morphology, similar to that of the Oriental, making it easily distinguishable from the Devon Rex, for instance.

Today, these cats enjoy unanimous approval and are as popular in Europe as in the United States. It should be said that, besides their original, purebred physique reminiscent of a greyhound's, they have a very pleasant character. Their athletic bodies, naturally alert and restless, are prone to all sorts of antics. These acrobats are always cheerful and are pleasant to live with. Generally sociable with their own kind and other animals, they loathe solitude and need company.

They are endowed with shrill, powerful voices. Their very short hair provides little protection against the elements and they are naturally sensitive to the cold, thus making them ideal candidates for apartment living. Affectionate and sensitive, they are close to their masters. Being of a highly prolific nature, they reproduce easily.

The fact that these cats virtually never molt greatly facilitates their masters' work.

Cornish Rex, black and white

DEVON REX

Other name: Poodle cats
Country of origin: Great Britain
Ancestors: Kirlee cat
Coat: short, fine, and soft, with dense and disorderly wavy fur
Colors: all

The Devon Rex is quite unusual, both in its curly fur and its unique expression that it owes to its huge eyes, high cheekbones, and low-set large ears, not unlike that of the famous "E.T." In kittens, it is only after several months that the coat takes on its typical wavy appearance. The density of the fur varies according to the part of the body; the hair is thicker on the under-parts (throat, chest, and stomach). Completely bald areas in the adult are penalized in competitions. All colors and patterns, with or without white markings, are authorized by the standard.

The Devon Rex is a breed that made a spontaneous appearance in the county of Devonshire, England, in 1960. In a litter of feral cats (domesticated cats that go back to being wild), Beryl Cox discovered a curly-haired kitten. Recalling the success of the Cornish Rex, which had come to light in a similar way in the neighboring region, she mated this cat with a stray tricolor cat. A male kitten from the litter, which she named Kirlee, also had a curly coat. After several unfruitful attempts at mating this cat and Cornish Rexes, the breeder tried a different tack, and Kirlee was outcrossed with British Shorthairs. As the gene responsible for the curly hair is recessive, extensive inbreeding was required to create the breed. Health problems inherent

Devon Rex, brown mackerel tabby

Devon Rex, blue cream mackerel tabby and white

in overly close crosses emerged, particularly the fatal hereditary disorder of spasticity. Serious efforts among breeders appear to have eradicated this, but vigilance is always called for and Devon Rex breeding remains highly scrupulous.

Today the breed is popular everywhere, including in the United States, and is established to the extent that only crosses between Devon Rexes are authorized.

Of medium size and "semi-cobby" body type, the Devon Rex has very short, curly fur, sparser in some areas, though not completely bald.

Alert and attentive, Devon Rexes are lively, playful cats. They are independent but sociable with their own kind or other animals and very affectionate with their masters. Moreover, they dislike being alone and require much attention. Their lack of thick fur means they are slightly sensitive to cold, thus making them highly suited to apartment living.

Like the Sphynx, the Devon Rex perspires through the skin, and its ears produce much wax. Regular cleansing using a wash glove and veterinary products specifically adapted to the ears are therefore recommended. As the short hair virtually never molts, maintenance is very easy.

European Shorthair, black silver blotched tabby

EUROPEAN SHORTHAIR

Other name: Swedish housecat
Country of origin: continental European countries
Ancestors: Egyptian and Syrian cats
Coat: short, dense, glossy, lying close to the body, without excessive undercoat
Colors: all, with the exception of colorpoint, chocolate, and lilac (corresponding to diluted chocolate)

Of medium size, the European Shorthair is a well-balanced cat with a fairly long body, which unlike the British Shorthair, lacks sturdiness. The head is slightly longer than it is wide, with rounded contours. Its large round eyes set well apart should have a color in keeping with that of the coat. The range of accepted colors is very wide.

As in most breeds, males are markedly larger and heavier than females.

Beware of offending this cat by calling it an "alley cat." The European Shorthair is a real feline breed, officially recognized since 1982, with a standard and pedigree.

The equivalent of the American Shorthair in the United States and the British Shorthair in England to which it is related, this cat belongs to a "natural" breed. Known from long ago, it is a probable descendant of Egyptian and Syrian cats, the ancestors of all of today's domestic cats, brought over to Europe with the Roman

Legions. Long ignored by breeders, rearing and selections began in the early 1980s.

The breed remains quite rare in Europe, except in Scandinavian countries, as it is still the victim of persistent confusion with ordinary nonpedigree cats. This breed therefore fails to rouse public interest, despite having undergone selections as severe as those of other breeds, in both physique and temperament. It has also been used in various selection programs with other breeds. The European Shorthair is not yet recognized by all cat federations and finds it hard to win acclaim. Only unions between European Shorthairs are authorized.

The first race standard was compiled in 1932, and the latest version dates from 1988. They describe an intermediate conformation-type cat, of medium size and solid build. The variety of colors possible constitutes a further asset for the breed.

Sharp and intelligent, European Shorthairs are rustic cats. Highly playful, they have inherited a resourceful character from their intrepid ancestors. They adapt well to any situation and demonstrate great ingenuity in sometimes quite unexpected situations! One of the boys, their good humor and intelligence make them pleasant and amusing companions. Affectionate and sociable, they are deeply attached to their masters. They will also tolerate other animals easily if raised to do so.

Gifted hunters, they like the outdoor life, but their capacity for adaptation means they are not confined to a particular dwelling—they are at home anywhere!

Maintenance is limited to a weekly brushing.

European Shorthair, brown blotched tabby

EXOTIC SHORTHAIR

Other name: Persian Shorthair
Country of origin: United States
Ancestors: American Shorthair and Persian
Coat: relatively long for a shorthaired cat, plush, dense, raised
Colors: all Persian colors are recognized: unicolor, parti-color, smoke, cameo, tabby, chinchilla, silver, golden shaded, colorpoint

Exotic Shorthair, tortoiseshell and white

This is a paradoxical cat as it resembles the Persian in all respects but its distinguishing feature—the fur. Rounded and sturdy, it is as powerful as its longhaired counterpart. The eyes are large and round, intense in color, giving it a soft, friendly expression. Like the Persian, it has a convex forehead and tiny snub nose. The tail is relatively short but is in proportion with the body length. The hair is slightly longer than that of other shorthaired cats, without lying against the body.

A purebred American, the Exotic Shorthair was born in the late 1950s and was officially recognized by the CFA in 1966. A chance creation at the outset as it occurred in the litters of American Shorthairs (which breeders crossed with Persians in the hope of obtaining a heavier figure and producing new colors), the breed finally underwent targeted selections with a view to becoming the Persian Shorthair. A few hybridizations with other breeds were included in the selection program, but outcrossings with other breeds are now prohibited, with the exception of the Persian, which remains fairly widespread in order to reinforce the type. Frequently found in the United States, the breed is also exported throughout the world.

Exotic Shorthairs are hard to breed, as any physical fault is immediately visible. Unlike in the Persian, the fur cannot be used to conceal anything! They therefore

Exotic Shorthair, brown spotted tabby

remain expensive to buy and show cats are highly prized.

The round and sturdy Exotic has inherited a gentle, quiet character from its Persian ancestor, though is a little more lively and playful.

These cats have the positive asset of being easy to live with. Sociable with their own kind, friendly with all the family without being exclusive in their relations, adaptable, discreet, and not very vocal, they can deal with any situation. They are at home anywhere, whether a house with garden or a city-dweller's apartment. The slight downside is that they do not take well to being left alone and need the contact and affection of their masters. They are generally good travelers.

Grooming requires only a decent weekly brushing. Frequent cleaning of the eyes is recommended using a physiological saline solution or a suitable veterinary product, as they tend to water. Extreme selections may end up weakening the breed; monitoring of the cats' health and diet is therefore important.

MAINE COON

Other name: Maine shag (longhair Maine)
Country of origin: United States (Maine)
Ancestors: local farm cats and Angora cats originating from Europe
Coat: medium, but uneven in length, silky with a light, fine undercoat. Shorter on the shoulders, the fur is longer on the flanks, the stomach, and the britches, and forms a sparse ruff. Considerable seasonal variations.
Colors: all except for chocolate, lilac, cinnamon, fawn, and the ticked tabby pattern

The Maine Coon is most probably the largest pedigree cat. Certain males may weigh more than 22 pounds (10 kilograms). The natural selection that forged the breed has led to robust individuals, capable of withstanding very harsh climatic conditions.

The body is long and substantial, very muscular and broad-chested. Medium in size, the head is slightly concave in profile, with no break, and sometimes with a slight hump on the tip of the nose. The eyes are large, with a slightly oblique setting. Tufts are desirable on the tips of the large ears and reinforce the cat's wild look. Though large, females are smaller than males. The breed's large build is related to a fairly late maturity—the cat is only really "finished" at around three or four years of age.

Legend has it that the Maine Coon is the product of the amorous adventures of a cat and raccoon, but it is more plausibly the fruit of unions between farm cats from the state of Maine in the United States, its native region, and cats imported from Europe by immigrants, including the Angoras that reached this region's coasts aboard merchant ships. These longhaired cats probably

Maine Coon, brown blotched tabby and white

mated with indigenous shorthaired cats and natural selection gave rise to the current breed.

Only the strongest individuals survived the severe winters, siring robust cats, capable of withstanding the region's harsh climatic conditions.

Considered to be the oldest natural American breed, it was initially highly prized for its rodent-hunting prowess. Then the breed went through a difficult period in the mid-twentieth century, outshone by more exotic cats such as the Persian or Siamese. Taken back in hand by enthusiastic breeders in the late 1960s, it gradually won back its initial status and was officially recognized by the CFA in 1974.

Today, the pedigree is enjoyed the world over. Its wild look and robust appearance have helped to establish its popularity.

Gentle giants, Maine Coons are calm, affectionate, and sociable cats, which make for easy living. Highly attached to their masters, they need space to maintain their athletic physique. Their natural resistance enables them to stay outdoors even when it's very cold.

Playful and athletic, Maine Coons are also well balanced and sociable. They do not take advantage of their size to compel recognition and, though often domineering, they are devoid of all aggressiveness.

The thin undercoat makes maintenance easy and a weekly brushing—slightly more sustained during molting—is sufficient.

Maine Coon, brown blotched tabby

MANDARIN

Other names: Oriental Longhair
Country of origin: United States
Ancestors: Oriental, Balinese
Coat: medium length, fine, silky, lying close to the body, with a light undercoat
Colors: all the colors of the Oriental: plain, tortie (tortoiseshell), tabby, silver, smoke, parti-color

The Mandarin follows a standard virtually identical to that of the Oriental, Siamese, and Balinese, with differences apparent only in the coat (length of hair and color) and, consequently, eye color. Its body type is that of a rangy, convex cat, yet is slightly heavier than an Oriental's. This impression is further reinforced by its medium-length hair forming a ruff around the neck, britches, and whipped tail. The hair is shorter on the head and shoulders. The eyes have an "Oriental-style" slant and are green in color. Blue eyes are the pre-rogative of white Mandarins.

The Mandarin is the result of a recent union between Orientals and Balinese (semi-longhair Siamese) performed in the United States with the clear aim of obtaining semi-longhair Orientals. We have thus come full circle, and there are now three Siamese "derivatives": the Oriental, the Balinese, and the Mandarin. The Mandarin was provisionally recognized in 1994, and a standard was compiled in 1998. A newcomer to the international ailurophile scene, this cat is still very rare in Europe but is attracting a growing number of fanciers.

With its green eyes (blue for white Mandarins), its Oriental look that is slightly less extreme than that of the original pedigree, and its medium-length fur, the

Mandarin, black

Mandarin is elegance incarnate. Svelte and refined, it is strong and muscular. It has a straight profile, with no break as is usual in such rangy, convex breeds.

Unions among the four varieties of Oriental cats are authorized and indeed necessary to fix the characteristics.

Calmer and more moderate than the shorthaired Oriental, Mandarins are nevertheless endowed with a strong personality. Lively and active, they are inveterate players and born explorers. There is no risk of boredom with these ever-cheerful cats. Like their ancestor the Siamese, they are vocal but have tuneful voices. They apply this ability to making themselves understood and attracting the attention of their beloved masters. Slightly less exclusive in their relations than the Siamese, they are nonetheless very close to their masters and like to be the center of attention. The flip side, as is to be expected, is that they hate solitude and require care and affection. Sociable and highly affectionate with their families, they appear slightly more reserved with strangers.

Maintenance is easy, given the light undercoat seldom prone to form hairballs. Weekly brushing—slightly more sustained during molting—is sufficient.

Mandarin, red mackerel tabby

Manx, blue spotted tabby

MANX

Other name: Isle of Man cat
Country of origin: Isle of Man
Coat: short, dense, with a very thick undercoat
Colors: all, with or without white

The Manx is distinguished by a spontaneous genetic mutation that results in the complete absence of a tail (the Rumpy Manx), in the persistency of one to three sacral vertebrae covered with hair (the Rumpy-riser Manx), or in the persistency of one to three caudal vertebrae forming a tail a few centimeters in length, often kinked (the Stumpy Manx). The inbreeding of cats on their native isle allowed this mutation to be perpetuated and to give rise to the breed. Besides this caudal anomaly, the Manx is characterized by its typical hopping gait (somewhat similar to that of a hare), due to its hind legs being longer than its forelegs.

The Manx developed on the Isle of Man, in the Irish Sea. Its exact origins are fairly hazy, with some maintaining that it is of Far Eastern ancestry. In any event, its island existence has allowed the development and preservation of a spontaneous genetic mutation affecting its tail and characterizing the breed.

The Manx was first noticed in Great Britain in the early twentieth century; the breed was then exported and is to be found everywhere today. A longhaired version recognized at a later date—the Cymric—has even evolved in the United States. In addition to unions between Manx cats, outcrossings are authorized with the Cymric and British Shorthair.

The Manx is appealing with its teddy-bear look, its compact, muscular body, its round head with full cheeks, and its very plush fur, an impression reinforced by the lack of tail. All coat colors—with or without white—are accepted.

Far from being handicapped by its tailless state, the Manx is a very active cat, as lithe and skillful as any other feline, as well as being a highly gifted hunter. Playful and cheery, they make for pleasant companions. They are sociable with other animals, patient with children, affectionate to their masters, and adaptable to all situations. Both breeders and owners praise their good nature and cheerful disposition. Easy to live with and intelligent, the Manx is a fine friend—robust and psychologically sound.

The main reservation concerning this pedigree lies in its reproduction and breeding, which are complicated due to low proliferation rates and the fact that all homozygous kittens (carrying the mutant allele twice) die in utero. In this case, two Manx Rumpies should not be mated, due to the lethal risk for the kittens. This is also why the standard authorizes outcrossings with British Shorthairs.

Maintenance is easy as the thick coat makes do with weekly brushing.

Manx, blue spotted tabby

EGYPTIAN MAU

Other name: Mau
Country of origin: Egypt
Ancestors: wildcats domesticated by the Egyptians (*Felis lybica ocreata*)
Coat: short, fine, silky, supple, lying close to the body
Colors: spotted tabby pattern in several varieties, including silver (silver base, black spots), bronze (bronze base, dark brown to black spots), and black smoke (smoke gray base, black spots). The basic coat carries at least two bands of ticking (alternating light and dark bands).

Egyptian Mau, black smoke

The Mau is the only natural domesticated breed of spotted cat. It also wears "makeup" and bears an "M" mark on its forehead, mascara lines on its cheeks, and rings on its tail, as well as on the chest and legs. Its distinctive color pattern is fascinating, and the contrast between the basic shade of its coat and that of the dappled markings further add to the particular impression it exudes. Graceful and elegant, the Mau also differs from other cats in its temperament and serenity.

The Mau (meaning "cat" in Egyptian) is directly descended from the first domesticated cats in Egypt, and traces of it appear in Egyptian mythology where it was venerated. The breed owes its recognition to the Russian princess Nathalie Troubetskoy who, at the end of World War II, brought some representatives of the breed first to Italy, then to the United States when she emigrated there in the late 1950s. The breed went on to develop in North America using new imports to avoid inbreeding. It was progressively recognized by the various cat associations and spread to the rest of the world, Europe in particular. Despite the fascination it holds for visitors to shows, the Mau is still not very widespread outside of the US.

Egyptian Mau, black silver spotted tabby

It is a natural breed, and no outcrossings with other races are permitted. Yet the Mau is itself at the origin of a large number of feline breeds.

Of medium size, it is a graceful, alert cat with a highly muscular body. Its head is as long as it is wide and carries large almond-shaped green eyes. The motifs on its coat stand out clearly due to the contrast between the ground color and that of the dappling.

Maus are well balanced both physically and mentally. Under no circumstances do they appear nervy or aggressive, and they detest agitation. The selective efforts of breeders have obtained a milder temperament, and today's Maus have both a wonderful physique and an easygoing personality.

Calm and reserved with strangers, they are conversely very close to their masters. Quite sociable with their own kind, they are cats that make for easy living, with a soft, melodious mewing and exemplary behavior. The only hitch is that they dislike being left alone and require much attention. Their quiet, reserved temperament does not stop them from being active and playful when the fancy takes them, and they appreciate a garden or space to work off surplus energy.

Their short hair is easy to maintain and requires only a weekly brushing.

Nebelung, blue

NEBELUNG

Other name: Medium-haired Russian Blue
Country of origin: United States
Ancestors: Russian Blue
Coat: dense, medium length, with a fairly fine undercoat.
Males have a fine ruff, which is less pronounced in females.
Colors: pale blue-gray, with silver tips. White is recognized
in this variety.

The Nebelung, a word of Germanic origin meaning "creature of the mist," is the medium-haired version of the Russian Blue. As such, it shares the same standard, with the exception of the coat. Like its relative, the Nebelung has a blue-gray coat, green eyes, and a head that is a modified wedge consisting of seven planes. The length and density of its fur give it a heavier appearance.

Tufts at the tips of the ears and britches are desirable. The length and density of the fur varies according to the season. As in the Russian Blue, the kittens may have ghost tabby markings that disappear as they grow up. Likewise, the green color of their eyes is only definitively established after a year.

The Nebelung's history is tied up with that of the Russian Blue, as this cat is its direct descendant. Medium-haired Russian Blues had already been observed more than a century ago, but at the time, they were considered undesirable within the breed and excluded from reproduction.

While American breeders were responsible for endeavoring to recreate and fix this variety, in the late 1980s it transpired that it was also bred in Russia, which may be proof of this breed's natural origin, as in the Russian Blue. The Nebelung is therefore a modern recreation of the medium-haired Russian Blue.

The first American specimens recorded under the Nebelung name, Siegfried and Brunhilde, were born in 1984 and 1985 respectively; they marked the breed's beginnings. They were then crossed with "natural" cats imported from Russia.

This new breed was officially recognized by TICA in 1987 as a medium-haired variety of the Russian Blue. They are still not very widespread today outside of the United States, Germany, the Netherlands, and Russia.

Unions between Nebelungs and Russian Blues are authorized. The hair length determines the breed to which the kittens belong.

In terms of temperament, Nebelungs are close to the Russian Blue. They are similarly shy and independent and dislike shouting and agitation. Affectionate and fairly exclusive in their relations with their masters, they appear suspicious of strangers.

Highly intelligent, they are reserved cats that refuse to be restrained and appear quite domineering and authoritarian. Yet once their trust is earned, they make wonderful, playful, and affectionate companions.

Their medium-length hair should be brushed regularly, and more frequently during spring and fall molting periods.

Nebelung, blue

Norwegian, red blotched tabby

NORWEGIAN

Other names: Norwegian Forest Cat, Skogkatt, Norwegian Wood Cat
Country of origin: Norway
Ancestors: Scandinavian cats
Coat: medium length, slightly oily texture, waterproof, glossy, with a woolly undercoat
Colors: all except colorpoint, chocolate, lilac, cinnamon, fawn, Burmese-type coloring (sepia). White markings are accepted in all colors.

The Norwegian is a large cat, with a long, sturdy body. From its Scandinavian origins, it has retained a robust constitution and fur, both dense and waterproof, to withstand anything. The ruff worn around the head gives it its typical appearance and adds to its wild look. The length and density of the fur varies considerably with the seasons; in summer, the coat is shorter and lacks a frontal bib. In cat shows, the quality of the fur is one of the judges' main criteria.

The Norwegian was born long ago in Scandinavia, where it is supposed to have accompanied the Vikings on their Drakkar boats. Norwegians lived in the wild before becoming farmyard cats. Around 1930, Norwegian breeders took an interest in the breed and started work on selections. The breed was recognized in 1972 and was progressively exported throughout the world, enjoying growing success.

This cat's initial appeal lies in its imposing build and thick fur—developed in order to adapt to the harsh climate of its region of origin—giving it a wild appearance. The triangular wedge head set at a slightly oblique angle with its almond-shaped eyes lends it a lively and intelligent expression. Tufts on the tips of the ears are desirable and further reinforce the wild impression emanating

Norwegian, blue blotched tabby

from this cat. The males are noticeably larger and heavier than the females and are characterized by a wider head.

The strong physique is combined with an assertive, self-confident character. Alert and dynamic, they require space and an outdoor life to be really happy. Apartment living is conceivable if they are able to go outside.

Easy to live with, Norwegians are pleasant companions, with well-balanced temperaments, able to adapt to all situations. Sociable with other animals, they are everyone's friend and good with children. Their splendid musculature makes them true athletes who excel at hunting. Lithe and robust, they are very good climbers. Like all well-built cats, they are fairly late in maturing (around four or five years).

Regular grooming is required to avoid the formation of hairballs. Weekly brushing—daily during molting—is therefore necessary.

OCICAT

Other name: Oci
Country of origin: United States
Ancestors: Siamese, Abyssinian
Coat: short, fine, smooth, satiny with a lustrous sheen
Colors: brown, chocolate, lilac, blue, cinnamon, fawn.
Silver varieties of these colors exist. All of these colors
are also authorized in colorpoint.

Ocicat, chocolate spotted tabby

The name "Ocicat"—a contraction of "ocelot" and "cat"—was given to this cat in reference to its resemblance to the wildcat. The breed owes this wild appearance to the color of its coat markings, and to its athletic, powerful bearing. The standard's preference goes to large cats, but it is most important that they remain well balanced and harmonious.

Each hair, except for the tip of the tail, carries alternating dark and light bands, a characteristic known as ticking. The ground color is fairly light, acting as a sharp foil to the darker markings. On the head, these markings form typical motifs (the "M" characteristic of tabbies, mascara lines around the eyes). Rings are present on the tail. White lockets are considered a fault.

The Ocicat was born in the United States, in the state of Michigan, in 1964, to the breeder Virginia Daly, quite by chance. A kitten with a distinctively marked coat appeared in a litter from a cross between a Siamese male and a Siamese-Abyssinian crossbred female—a union performed initially with the idea of obtaining tabby point Siamese. The result encouraged breeders to try out different outcrossings, with the aim of reproducing such a cat and fostering the resemblance with the ocelot.

Siamese, Orientals, Abyssinians, Egyptian Maus, and even American Shorthairs were used and, in the course of the crosses and selections, the Ocicat

Ocicat, chocolate spotted tabby

pedigree was established. The United States officially recognized it in 1986, to be followed by the other cat associations. All unions with other breeds—notably with Abyssinians—are now prohibited. This cat is still not widespread outside of the US.

The wild appearance, provided by the spotted tabby coat with sharply contrasting marks, is further reinforced by its athletic profile and natural strength. The head is as long as it is wide. Tufts at the tips of the ears are desirable. The body type is semi-cobby and highly muscular.

Ocicats are wild in appearance only, as they possess mild temperaments. Sociable and affectionate, they are also very playful and affectionate. Forever curious, they are real explorers.

The Siamese legacy is loyalty and a somewhat exclusive attachment to their masters. Markedly less vocal than their cousins, they are easy to live with. They adapt very quickly to new living conditions, but find solitude hard to cope with. They tend to be domineering toward their own kind.

Their short, fine hair is easily maintained through weekly brushing.

Oriental, white

ORIENTAL

Other name: Oriental Shorthair
Country of origin: Thailand
Coat: short, dense, fine, silky, lying close to the body
Colors: many, classified in several varieties: solid,
as in the white Oriental (the only one to have blue eyes);
parti-color; tortie (or tortoiseshell) and derivatives; smoke; tabby

Like the Siamese, a breed with similar origins, the Oriental represents the archetypal rangy, convex feline, the greyhound of the cat world. The impression of a long head is reinforced by the absence of break on its straight profile. The almond-shaped eyes are slanted and are emerald green in color. The legs and tail are long and slender. Despite its finesse, the cat exudes a sense of strength due to its long, firm musculature.

Like the Siamese, the Oriental originates from Thailand, the breed's characteristics having subsequently been determined in England. It is hard to say which of the two cats precedes the other. Some maintain that the Siamese is the original type, with the Oriental being a deliberate creation resulting from a quite specific breeding program.

Arriving in Britain in the 1920s, Thai cats underwent selections that gave rise to Siamese and the first Orientals. The Siamese swiftly gained the upper hand over their cousins, and it was not until 1950 that British breeders really began to take an interest in Orientals.

Crosses between Siamese and European cats of various hues led to the establishment of the Oriental's current range of colors.

In the early 1970s, the breed was introduced in the United States, which would develop its own selection programs, with breeders favoring an extreme rangy type while the English remained more moderate. The breed was officially recognized in 1972. The longhaired variety, the Oriental Longhair or Mandarin, was approved in 1994.

Orientals remain considerably less widespread than Siamese, who continue to steal the limelight from them. Yet both breeds are very close, and their standards are virtually identical, save a few details, notably with respect to the colors of the coat and, by extension, of the eyes.

In terms of temperament, Orientals are also very close to Siamese, although perhaps a touch less exclusive. Both are very lively and extroverted. Affectionate and possessive with their masters, they know how to attract attention by loud, continuous mewing if necessary. Sociable and playful, they do not take well to being alone and detest indifference. They need to be fully involved in family life and will make this quite clear if need be.

They are formidable hunters outdoors. Their slenderness, combined with their agility and impressive musculature, mean that they excel in this activity. They reproduce easily due to their sexual precocity and their prolific nature.

Their short hair is easy to maintain and regular brushing suffices.

Oriental, chocolate

PERSIAN

Other name: Longhair
Country of origin: England
Ancestors: Oriental Angora cats
Coat: long over the whole body, dense, fine, silky, with an abundant undercoat that reinforces the impression of volume
Colors: all; more than two hundred possible colors

The Persian is characterized by its long, dense fur and compact body type, and its very distinctive facial appearance, with a broad, sometimes slightly snub nose and a clearly defined break located between two round eyes. Its ears are small, further reinforcing the compact impression given by this cat.

Round and stocky, it has relatively short limbs. It cuts a majestic figure, and its fur is the longest of all pedigree cats (the hair length averages nearly 4 inches [10 centimeters] but can double around the ruff). The range of coat colors is very wide with more than two hundred varieties including solid, tortie, smoke, bicolor, tabby, and chinchilla, as well as derivatives such as the Persian colorpoint, known as Himalayan in the United States.

The world's most famous cat, topping the breed popularity rankings, was born in Great Britain in the late nineteenth century.

The quest for longhaired cats is not recent, and Europeans sought to obtain such cats very early on. The first attempts at selection were made in Italy, where Angora cats were imported from Persia (present-day Iran), whence the breed's subsequent name.

British breeders worked on selections using Angora cats from France and Italy and autochthonous individuals. The majority of these cats were of Oriental

Persian, red self

Persian, Brown mackerel tabby

origin, as the Turkish Angora had existed since the sixteenth century. The first subjects resulting from this selection were exhibited in London in 1871. This show was to mark the beginnings of a rigorous breeding program. Breeders set about widening the range of possible colors—and succeeded as more than two hundred varieties are listed today! The stockiest and most compact cats were systematically selected, an extreme type even more sought-after in the United States. Persians have been called upon in the creation of several breeds of cat, notably the Sacred Cat of Burma.

Their temperament goes well with their round, soft-looking physique, as Persians are naturally gentle and placid. Rather sedentary, they are perfect candidates for apartment living, which quite befits their character. Friendly and sociable, they are devoid of all aggressiveness and are very affectionate with their entourage. They have no difficulty in accepting their own kind and other comrades of all shapes and sizes. Discreet and of few words, Persians make for fine companions who need peace and quiet to be fully contented. And, unlike other breeds, they cope relatively well with being left alone.

These round, stocky cats mature quite late and their reproduction is generally rather difficult as their body type often leads to problems during birthing.

The fur requires careful, regular grooming as its thickness is conducive to the formation of hairballs. It should therefore be untangled on a daily basis. In addition, molting can be quite impressive. An extremely compact body type may lead to certain abnormalities in the tear ducts and is manifested by ocular discharge. The eyes should therefore be cleaned regularly if necessary.

Above: Persian, dilute calico
Facing page: Persian, white

PIXIE-BOB

Country of origin: United States
Ancestors: Bobcat (small North American lynx), American farm cat
Coat: shorthaired variety: soft, woolly hair, springy to the touch, not lying too close to the body, and longer on the stomach; longhaired variety: hair lying more closely to the body, very soft, maximum length 2 inches (5 centimeters)
Colors: all shades of brown spotted tabby with strong inverted ticking (darker bands toward the skin and lighter at the tips of the hair). Spots are arranged randomly.

Shorthair Pixie-Bob, brown spotted

The Pixie-Bob is a large cat with a wild look, and a substantial, muscular, and powerful body. The breed consists of two varieties according to hair length. The head is typically an inverted pear-shape, with a hooked nose, a firm chin, and brick-red nose leather. The eyes are heavily lidded, giving a slightly sleepy appearance. If possible, the ears have tufts at the tips, thereby emphasizing the resemblance with the lynx. The bobbed tail is naturally short, with a minimum length of 2 inches (5 centimeters), but should not exceed the hock. Polydactyly is accepted in this breed, as the relatively large paws can have up to seven digits. Unions between two polydactyl cats are, however, prohibited to avoid establishing this feature—which is tolerated but not desirable—in the breed.

The density of the hair varies according to the season. In winter, the thickness intensifies the ticking (alternating light and dark bands) and gives the impression that the coat is dusted with frost. A white medallion; overly long ruff or hair for the longhaired variety; a lack of ticking; or a tail that is too short or full are faults penalized in shows.

Longhair Pixie-Bob, brown spotted tabby

The Pixie-Bob was born from a breeding program initiated in the United States in the early 1980s with the aim of creating a domestic cat resembling a small North American lynx, the bobcat. A breeder from Washington State, Carol Ann Brewer, set about doing so by mating individuals born of outcrossings between domestic cats and bobcats. She kept those kittens that possessed bobcat characteristics. One of the products of these unions between domestic cats and bobcats, a polydactyl female called Pixie, is considered to be the breed's mother.

The Pixie-Bob was progressively recognized by the American cat federations, and the majority of its representatives are concentrated in the United States.

Its wild look—strongly reminiscent of its ancestor, the lynx—is not in keeping with its soft, docile character.

Playful and very affectionate, Pixie-Bobs are tolerant with children and highly attached to their masters. They appear a little more reserved with strangers.

They make for easy cats to live with, discreet and good-natured. Calm and thoughtful, they do not need to express themselves to make themselves understood, and they say relatively little. With their large build, these cats are slow developers and do not mature until two or three years old.

Shorthaired Pixie-Bob fur requires only minimal grooming. The longhaired variety should be brushed at a slightly more sustained pace.

RAGDOLL

Country of origin: United States (California)
Ancestors: Persian, Burmese
Coat: medium length, diaphanous, silky, little undercoat
Colors: colorpoint, mitted or gloved (Siamese pattern with gloves at the tips of the four paws and a white chin), bicolor (colorpoint with white extensions)

Like the Siamese, the Ragdoll is a colorpoint breed of cat but of large build with medium-length fur. It is characterized by its extreme mildness, at times verging on an absence of reaction. It is late in maturing, around three or four years. A ruff is preferred. The eyes are of the most vivid possible blue, regardless of coat color.

This large cat was born in the United States in the 1960s through selections by breeder Ann Baker who, though the origins remains unattested, most probably crossed Persians with Burmese, selecting the subjects as she went along. Once the type was established, the breed was recognized in the US in 1965 and was then exported to Europe. Today the breed is well developed in the United States but remains limited elsewhere.

Besides its large format, this cat stands out with its three varieties of color: bicolor, colorpoint, and mitted. In the mitted pattern, the Ragdoll is distinguished from the Burmese by the presence of a white chin and sometimes a white blaze on the nose or between the eyes, which is accepted in the standard. Its nose is also longer, its ears more rounded, and its eyes more oval-shaped. It has medium-length fur that is shorter on the face and forepaws. The tail should be as long as the body.

The size of this cat is impressive, with some males weighing in at around 22 pounds (10 kilograms). Thus,

Ragdoll, seal point

the Ragdoll exudes an impression of strength. Yet this strength is well under control, and the name "Ragdoll" sums up its character—very gentle, compounded by its low muscle tone. Ragdolls therefore make perfect family pets, good-natured toward all. They are evidently ideal with children—but the kids need to be taught to respect the cat, as Ragdolls are tolerant to the extreme! Easygoing homebodies, they are better suited to apartment living. Loving and sometimes even clingy, they are very attached to their masters.

They get on well with their own kind and other animals but do not like being left alone.

This cat's large size correlates with slow growth, only reaching its final size around three or four years old. Particular care is needed with regard to diet during growth. Despite its abundant nature, the fur is fairly easy to maintain as, due to the virtual absence of undercoat, it seldom gets tangled and makes do with weekly brushing.

Ragdoll, blue bicolor

Sacred Cat of Burma, seal tabby

SACRED CAT OF BURMA

Other name: Birman

Country of origin: France

Ancestors: Lao Tsun temple cats, Burma, according to legend; more plausibly a Siamese with white markings on the extremities and a longhaired cat

Coat: medium length, silky, with little undercoat

Colors: pigmented coat on the extremities, as in the Siamese, with gloved paws; the dark markings may take various shades (seal point, chocolate point, red point), and the rest of the coat ranges from white to cream

With its semi-long hair, colorpoint pattern (designating a light body and darker extremities), and its eyes of sapphire blue, the Birman stands for elegance and feline beauty. Of medium size, it nonetheless exudes an impression of strength, with its relatively stocky, substantial body, reinforced by its dense, silky hair of medium length.

The kittens are almost entirely white when born; the coloring of the extremities and the white gloves do not appear until the age of one or two months. The coat darkens slightly with age. A very particular feature of this breed is the white "gloving" of the feet. These gloves end in an even line on the forepaws but are lengthened by "laces" on the back legs.

The Birman's origins remain hazy. Some maintain that the breed comes from cats imported from Burma in the 1920s, while for others it emerged directly in France. In any event, it was indeed in France that the breed developed and selection was implemented; the first individuals were shown in the 1930s.

The Birman's powers of seduction lie primarily in its physique but are backed up by its wonderful character. Midway between the temperament of the Persian and the Siamese, Birmans are quiet, well-balanced cats. A full-fledged member of the family, they are very affectionate and need to be fully involved in household activities. They do not like to be kept out of things or to be left alone! And they are also a touch possessive. Highly playful, they enjoy the company of children and that of other cats or other animals, with which they generally cohabit well. Quite vocal, they present no bother to their entourage, as their voices are soft and melodious. A perfect cat for apartment life, they are also very much at ease outside, where they can try out their hunting talents.

Breeders refer to the Birman as a "moderate cat in all respects." Far from being pejorative, this definition aptly describes the cat's poised, well-balanced character, playful without going to extremes, loving but not lacking in character, and not fussy about food.

Maintenance is simple, as a weekly brushing suffices. In short, the Sacred Cat of Burma makes for easy living!

Sacred Cat of Burma, seal point

SAVANNAH

Country of origin: United States
Ancestors: Serval and domestic cats
Coat: short to medium length, lying close to the body, very particular feel to the fur—partly rough but softer at the spots, with a silky undercoat
Colors: spotted tabby pattern, with invariably black spots and a variable ground color depending on whether the Savannah is brown spotted tabby, black, black silver, or black smoke (in this case the tabby "ghost" markings remain nonetheless clearly visible)

Savannah, brown spotted

The Savannah is characterized by its wild appearance, a legacy from its direct relative the Serval (a small African wildcat). Both are rangy and large in size. The Savannah's elongated body is in stark contrast to its typically small head. Its large ears are high-set, and its fairly short tail, thick and ringed, has a black tip. The fur has a quite particular feel. The markings on the coat are round and elongated to different degrees but are always black regardless of the ground color, which generally varies from golden to orange. The stomach is systematically spotted.

The Savannah is the result of a cross between an African wildcat, the Serval, and domestic cats with spotted coats. The breeders' aim was to produce a large domestic cat with the characteristics of its wild cousin. The first hybridizations were performed in the United States in the early twentieth century. The Serval's aesthetic qualities and its docile character determined the breeders' decision to cross it with domestic cats.

The breed remains limited, with only a few hundred subjects throughout the world, and breeding is the domain of professionals skilled in controlling lineages and hybridizations. The standard's rigor and precision provide a sound guarantee to avoid derivatives and

Savannah, brown spotted

allow the Savannah to conserve the nearest possible appearance to that of the Serval.

The Savannah's look sets it in a class of its own in the cat world. The body is very long, characterized by a deep rib cage and slightly raised hindquarters with somewhat oversized hips and upper legs. The small wedge-shaped head has well-spaced eyes, ideally adorned with a typical white mascara. Eye color is intense, varying from gold to green.

Although wild, the Serval is a cat with remarkable facilities for adaptation, cohabiting relatively well with humans, even to the point of fairly often being domesticated. Savannahs—first generations included—are therefore immediately gentle and sociable. However, cats are not authorized for show until after the third generation.

Affectionate and intelligent, Savannahs are very well adapted to domestic life and exhibit no aggressiveness, even in the first generations. They can just be a little shy at times and reserved with strangers. The following generations present all the characteristics of perfect domestic cats, sociable and good-natured toward all. Moreover, any sign of aggressiveness is liable for disqualification from cat shows.

The Savannah belongs to a breed of cat whose short coat is easy to maintain.

SCOTTISH FOLD

Other name: Highland Fold (for the longhaired variety)
Country of origin: Scotland
Ancestors: female barn cat, British Shorthair
Coat: short, thick, tight fitting, very dense, resilient, with a thick undercoat
Colors: all

The Scottish Fold is distinguished from its fellow cats by the very distinctive form of its ears, folded forward, giving the appearance of wearing a natural cap. This characteristic is due to the dominant "fold" gene. This mutation, known as "folded ear," first appeared in Scotland and led to the Scottish Fold breed. It was subsequently selected to create other breeds, including the

Highland Fold, the longhaired variety of the Scottish. Unions between two cats who are bearers of the mutation are likely to cause abnormality in the skeleton and are therefore prohibited. Thus, Scottish Folds are crossed with British Shorthairs, British Longhairs, or American Shorthairs.

The other characteristic feature of the Scottish Fold is the rounded, quite stocky appearance that it shares with its ascendant the British Shorthair. The typical morphology of the ears is not visible before the age of one month.

As its name suggests, the Scottish Fold hails from Scotland. The mutation that led to the characteristic shape of its ears was first observed in 1961 on a female barn cat named Susie. Her unions with British Shorthairs produced kittens bearing the same mutation. Nonetheless, unions between Folds obtained in this way revealed abnormalities in the skeleton, leading to the suspension of selections. They were relaunched in the United States in 1971, with outcrossings including British, American, and Exotic Shorthairs. The American federations finally acknowledged the breed, and immediate success accompanied this formal recognition. In the early 1980s, the breed returned to Europe but, still unrecognized by all cat federations, remains much less widespread there. Outcrossings with Persians made it possible to create a semi-long variety called Highland Fold. German breeders, crossing the breed with cats bearing the Rex mutation, created the Poodle Cat, which combines curly fur with drooping ears.

The Scottish Fold is a short, well-rounded cat, stocky and robust. The head is no exception to this overall impression as it is round with full cheeks. The ears are small, bent forward, with single or double folds.

This well-rounded aspect is also present in the Fold's character. They are playful cats, easy to live with, and devoid of all aggressiveness. Affectionate and not very vocal, they are well suited to apartment living and tolerate their masters' absence as long as they receive enough attention on their return. These big sensitive souls get on well with other animals but need peace and quiet to be fully contented.

The Fold's thick fur is maintained through weekly brushing—slightly more sustained during molting.

Scottish Fold, tortoiseshell

SELKIRK REX

Other name: Rex Selkirk
Country of origin: United States
Ancestors: Persian, American female alley cat
Coat: shorthaired or longhaired variety, plush, dense fur, curly like that of a sheep, with a thick undercoat
Colors: all

Shorthair Selkirk Rex, blue point

A rounded, heavy-boned cat, the Selkirk is distinguished by its curly hair, quite different from that of the Devon Rex or Cornish Rex, which is much longer and denser. There are two registered varieties: the shorthaired and longhaired. The many curls are well delineated in both cases, particularly at neck, stomach, and tail level. The degree of curl in the fur is not constant but varies according to season, climate, and the cat's state of health. Kittens are born curled but, as they grow, the curls slacken and then curl back; the fur only takes on its definitive appearance around the age of two years.

The Selkirk appeared very recently in the United States. Like that of most breeds of cat with such striking characteristics, its birth was a matter of chance. A small female in Wyoming in 1988 was found to have curly hair. It was adopted by a reputed breeder of Persians who mated it with one of her own cats, a black Persian. Some of the kittens sired were born with curly hair. The mutation responsible for the hair's curly appearance is a spontaneous one borne by a dominant gene, unlike the genes responsible for the curly hair of the Devon Rex or Cornish Rex.

The breeder continued the outcrossings, and the breed was born after a decade or so. Its name refers to the mountains in which the original little matriarch named Miss de Pesto was found.

Longhair Selkirk Rex, blue cream and white

The recent creation of this pedigree has forced breeders to use other breeds—notably the American Shorthair and the Persian—to establish it and to obtain a sufficient number of lineages. Today, only unions between Selkirks are authorized.

Selkirks are medium-sized cats of semi-cobby body type, strong and with abundant fur. The head is rounded with heavy jowls. Although descended from the Persian, they should not present a nose break. All coat colors are authorized, regardless of coat length (short or medium length), but well-defined shades are preferred.

Despite their fluffy teddy-bear appearance, Selkirks are active and playful cats that like to work off their energy. Sociable with other animals, they are affectionate and well balanced. Like Persians, they are gentle and get on well with children. Easy to live with, they are highly adaptable and can be fully contented in an apartment as long as they receive enough care and attention.

Despite its density, the fur is relatively easy to maintain; the coat should not be brushed too often as this may damage the curls.

SIAMESE

Other names: Colorpoint Shorthair, Royal Cat of Siam
Country of origin: Thailand
Ancestors: sacred cats from the temples of Siam (according to one hypothesis)
Coat: short, soft, fine, shiny, and close fitting
Colors: chocolate, seal, blue, or lilac. Also possible: tabby, tortie, or silver. Bicolor coats exist (white markings in the points and on the body).

The Siamese has a rangy body and a wedge-shaped head, in the highly characteristic "Y" shape with an elongated muzzle, almond-shaped eyes, and wide ears. The eyes are the most vivid blue possible. Not all Siamese squint; when the condition does exist, it is not constant.

Breeders initially sought to obtain a kinked tail (the "Siamese knot"), but this conformation is now considered a fault and tends to be eradicated after the appropriate selective crosses.

And far from being limited to the classic seal point coat, the Siamese can come in more than three hundred different shades, combining coat color and all possible characteristics (silver, tabby, bicolor). At birth, kittens are white or cream, and the motifs become established progressively.

The Siamese is one of the oldest breeds of cat and may be traced to Thailand, its birthplace, from the fourteenth century. Everything about it is fine and graceful: the body is long and lithe, with a slender tapered tail, and the head is narrow. It is impossible to remain indifferent to the Siamese with its strange gaze—fascinating or disturbing—and its distinctive husky mewing that some consider unfriendly.

Siamese, seal tabby point and white

Siamese have tough characters. They are bold and fearless, even if they may appear aloof to strangers. They are full of energy and, unlike many of their fellow creatures, are not made for spending long hours asleep in their baskets. They may be termed active.

Lovers of cats with personality will delight in having a Siamese at their side. Indeed, they are not your everyday cats. They have a reputation for being vocal. It is true that they like to express themselves, whether they are satisfied or discontent. One thing is sure—they are demonstrative and know how to make themselves understood!

Solitude is not their cup of tea, and as they are not independent spirits, they will demand attention if they feel neglected. Sensitive souls, they may become depressed if forsaken. Very close to their masters, to whom they vow unlimited admiration, they are possessive and do not hesitate to show their jealousy! For amateurs of the breed, the Siamese is the most dog-like of all cats. This dependence toward their families is also shown in their great sensitivity. Highly intelligent, they are easy to train and appear sociable with the various members of their entourage.

The short coat, fine and close fitting, does not require much maintenance.

Siamese, seal point

Siberian, brown mackerel tabby and white

SIBERIAN

Other names: Sibi, Siberian Cat
Country of origin: Russia
Ancestors: cats native to Siberia
Coat: medium to long, bushy, luxuriant, and waterproof, with a thick undercoat
Colors: all, except for chocolate and lilac

The Siberian is an example of a natural breed that has evolved on its own, initially living in the wild in a particular geographical region—in this case, Russia. Siberians have retained a visible hardiness from these origins, exuding an impression of strength and power.

The thick, waterproof fur provides protection against harsh climes. The breed is slow to mature, completing its development at around four or five years of age. They are stockier than the Maine Coon and have a rounder head than the Norwegian's.

A large, sturdy, and compact cat, the Siberian has lived in the wild since ancestral times. The rustic physique and thick, insulating fur testify to a past in lands with a harsh climate. Despite these indisputable Russian origins, it was in Germany that breeding really got underway on the initiative of Hans and Betty Schultz, who imported the first specimens and set about developing the breed. The United States imported these cats in the late 1980s.

The breed is well established today and is no longer confused with the Maine Coon or the Norwegian, which both have origins, hair type, and physique similar to the Siberian's.

The Siberian is a medium-sized cat that appears larger due to its heavy, stocky, and highly muscular body and the thickness of its fur. This impression of strength is nonetheless mitigated by the sweet expression given by the rounded head and large, slightly slanting eyes. The body has a characteristic "barrel-shaped" form due to the fullness of the ribs. The hair comprises a triple coat: the primary guard coat, awn hairs, and undercoat. It forms a ruff at the back of the head.

Still very rare outside of Russia and Germany, Siberians are nonetheless cats that make for easy living, symbolizing a "quiet force." Active and playful when the fancy takes them, they are calm and peaceful at other times during the day, and are even known to laze around on the couch! However, these rustic cats need space and an outdoor life to be fully contented. Their thick fur has to live up to its protective role!

Sociable with their own kind and other animals, Siberians are affectionate and close to their masters, tending to follow them everywhere. Robust and active, they make good hunters and unparalleled climbers.

Despite its thickness, the fleece is fairly easy to maintain, making do with a weekly brushing—daily during molting season.

Siberian, Neva Masquerade blue tabby

SINGAPURA

Other name: Kucinta (in Singapore)
Country of origin: Singapore
Ancestors: cats native to Singapore city, initially living semi-wild
Coat: short, fine, with no undercoat, lying close to the body
Colors: ticked coat—ivory ground; light beige muzzle, stomach, and throat; ticking (several light and dark alternating bands on each hair shaft), brown cosmetic markings, and bars on the insides of the forefeet and on the knees

The Singapura is known for being the smallest breed of cat in the world. It weighs less than 7 pounds (3 kilograms), and has a compact appearance. The ticked coat is a further distinguishing feature. The rather small head is typical in form with its huge, bright eyes and large ears.

The Singapura is aptly named as it does indeed hail from Singapore, where its ancestors have lived in a semi-wild state since ancient times.

In the mid-1970s, this miniature cat captivated a couple of American tourists, Tommy and Hal Meadows, during their stay in the city; they imported the first specimens to California in 1975. These breeders of Siamese were soon won over and had more shipped out. With the successive imports, the breed developed in the US. Some cat historians mention unions with the Burmese to establish the pedigree. In any event, the definitive Singapura type was recognized as a breed in the 1980s. Since then, cats have been exported throughout the world, particularly to France and Great Britain, where they have been known since 1989. Relatively widespread in the United States, the Singapura has not become dominant elsewhere, remaining a limited breed.

Designated a National Treasure in Singapore, these cats are primarily appealing in their physique, with their miniature body type, ticked coat, and large expressive eyes.

Despite its wild origins, the Singapura is a very gentle cat, highly attached to its masters. Curious and sociable, they are not very "talkative" but have melodious voices. They are playful and have preserved their cynegetic instincts—with a Singapura in the house, mice should watch out! If there are several cats together, they hunt in packs, in the style of wolves, a vestige of their ancestral culture. Moreover, they are quick to initiate other household cats to this form of hunting and to shared games.

An inordinate taste for hunting does not stop these small felines from being the ideal companion, affectio-nate and cuddly, ever prone to climbing onto their masters' shoulders and with a tendency to follow them around everywhere!

They are able to adapt to apartment living provided that they receive sufficient attention and are not left out, as they are sensitive souls.

The short coat is very easy to maintain. Regular brushing suffices.

Snowshoe, bicolor

SNOWSHOE

Other name: Snow-Shoe

Country of origin: United States

Ancestors: Siamese, bicolor American Shorthair

Coat: short, thick, glossy, lying close to the body, with little undercoat

Colors: all the classic Siamese colors (seal, blue, chocolate, lilac), in two varieties: mitted (white on no more than a third of the body) and bicolor (white does not exceed two-thirds of the body)

The Snowshoe is a colorpoint cat that combines the color of the Siamese with the white-gloved feet of the Sacred Cat of Burma. Larger and heavier than the Siamese, it is a cat of medium size, with a sense of power and elegance. It is distinguished by its colorpoint pattern, along with feet with white paws and the presence of an inverted "V" mark on the face.

The Snowshoe has a characteristic coloring, with points noticeably darker than the rest of the body and, if possible, of even color. Ideally, the white gloving is regular on all four feet and, in all cases, should not go more than halfway up the foot on the forepaws and mid-thigh level on the hind legs. Like the Siamese, the eyes are an intense blue.

At birth, Snowshoe kittens are white, as the points only appear with age. Tabby ghost markings are also sometimes found on young cats, but disappear as they grow up.

As with all colorpoints, the ground color tends to darken as the cat gets older.

The Snowshoe is a recent breed, which emerged in the United States in the 1960s. Aiming to produce white-gloved Siamese, the breeder Dorothy Hinds-Daugherty, based in Philadelphia, crossed moderate-type (not very Oriental-looking) Siamese with bicolor American Shorthairs. A few Birmans were also added to the cocktail shaker that led to the breed being established.

Officially recognized by TICA in the 1980s, the breed remains limited outside of the United States. In its physique, the Snowshoe combines the heavy appearance of the American Shorthair with the length and elegance of Orientals.

Endowed with a sturdy character, the Snowshoe is a lively, playful cat. Powerful and agile, they are excellent hunters. They are reputed for being sociable with their own kind and with dogs.

Less exclusive than the Siamese in their relations, they are more demonstrative and talkative than the American Shorthair. A well-balanced compromise between the two breeds, Snowshoes make for pleasant and affectionate companions, attached to their masters. Tolerant with children, they share in their games but know where to stop. Gentle and less demanding than their Siamese relatives, they are easy cats to live with.

The short hair is not difficult to maintain so weekly brushing is sufficient.

Snowshoe, bicolor

SOKOKE

Sokoke, brown mackerel tabby

Other name: African Shorthair
Country of origin: Kenya
Ancestors: wildcats from the Sokoke Forest, Kenya: Khadzonzo
Coat: very short, lying close to the body, shiny, with no undercoat
Colors: brown, marble, tabby

Slim and of medium size, the Sokoke is the image of a miniature wildcat, both in its bearing and in its marbled coat. The head appears small for the body. Tufts at the tips of the ears, as in the Lynx, are desirable. The Sokoke's fur is very short and glossy, without being silky. Only the color tabby marbled with brown or black and an "agouti" coat (streaked with alternate light and dark bands) are authorized. The tip of the tail is systematically black. No white markings are tolerated on the head or body.

Still extremely rare outside of their country of origin, Sokokes are a natural breed as they are direct descendants of an African wildcat, the Khadzonzo, which lives in the tropical Sokoke Forest in Kenya. An Englishwoman, Jeni Slater, was living in Kenya when she discovered a litter of kittens on her plantation in 1978, and first domesticated this cat. Enchanted by their slenderness and their distinctive coat, she began breeding them. One of her Danish friends likewise fell under the spell and took a couple back to her homeland. Through subsequent selective importations aimed at strengthening the population and reducing inbreeding, the breed became established in Europe. The pedigree was officially recognized in 1993 but remains very scarce.

Very slender and of medium size, Sokokes are elegant cats, not unlike the ocelot. High on the legs, they

Sokoke, brown mackerel tabby

have relatively small heads for their bodies. Their large, luminous eyes, ranging from amber to light green in color, give them a gentle and intelligent expression. The top of the skull is almost flat. Only unions between Sokokes are authorized.

For a feline directly descended from wildcats, the Sokoke has a rather easygoing, friendly character. Sociable with other animals—other cats as well as dogs—and affectionate with their masters, they make pleasant and mild-mannered companions. Yet they are not bereft of personality . . . or of muscular tone! Lively and agile, they are true all-around athletes: climbers, swimmers, and runners. As such, they require space and

life in the open air; they would be miserable if confined to a small apartment and unable to go outside. Though quite vocal, they are no nuisance as they have soft and melodious voices. Friendly with children, they are affectionate with all the family, but this does not stop them from being rather independent on the whole. They enjoy their own company and are never clingy.

The very short hair, virtually devoid of undercoat, is very easy to maintain; weekly brushing suffices.

SOMALI

Other names: Longhaired Abyssinian
Country of origin: Canada
Ancestors: Abyssinians
Coat: moderate length, dense, resilient, very fine, soft
Colors: ticking on the hair shaft (alternating dark and light bands, ending with a dark band), several colors possible: ruddy, blue, sorrel (cinnamon), beige fawn, silver black, silver sorrel, silver blue

Somali, ruddy

The Somali is a longhaired variety of the Abyssinian, which it greatly resembles, particularly in summer when the fur is less dense. The almond-shaped eyes, yellow to hazel in color, look as if they are wearing eyeliner. The ticking of each hair shaft intensifies the coat's color. Initially limited to ruddy and sorrel, the range of hues has developed and many shades are authorized today, particularly in Europe.

The Somali has had difficulties in becoming established, its history merging with that of the Abyssinian. Kittens with semi-long hair appeared spontaneously in the litters of Abyssinians, to the great displeasure of breeders who were quick to exclude them from reproduction, even getting rid of them! That is, until a Canadian breeder decided to keep the nonstandard cats and present them at a cat show. American and Canadian breeders pursued her work and set about developing the Somali as a breed in its own right, by fixing the semi-long hair in the Abyssinian. The breed was finally recognized in the late 1960s.

In reference to their Abyssinian ancestors, they compete in the "shorthaired" category in cat shows. Furthermore, unions between Somalis and Abyssinians are still authorized.

Medium in size, Somalis are elegant and rangy cats.

Their ticked, semi-long hair is their original feature, and males may even wear a ruff around the neck. The coat color and quality of the fur are prime concerns in breeding. Ticking is not present at birth and kittens have very dark coats. As it appears progressively, the definitive coat color remains undetermined for several months. The fur's appearance also changes according to the season; it is denser in winter.

The Somali has a well-balanced character and knows how to pace its energy. Active and dynamic, Somalis are nonetheless calmer than their Abyssinian brothers and appear very loving toward their masters, whom they generally follow everywhere, without being clingy or possessive.

Very playful, they are true athletes who like to work off surplus energy outdoors. Fanciers are unanimous in acknowledging the intelligence of this cat, able to adapt to any situation.

Weekly brushing is sufficient to maintain the coat, but should be more frequent during molting.

Somali, sorrel

SPHYNX

Other name: Canadian Hairless
Country of origin: Canada, then Europe
Coat: hairless skin or light persistent down, "peach skin" in texture, particularly soft to the touch
Colors: all

Sphynx, harlequin brown blotched tabby

The Sphynx is not really nude as its skin is very often covered with a fine down. Besides its lack of hair, this cat is characterized by its large ears (very wide at the base) and big oval eyes that are well spaced. The skin is wrinkled. The tail may have a tuft of hair at its tip (lion tail). Some hairs may persist on the face, the tail, and the testicles.

Hated by some and adored by others, the Sphynx leaves no one indifferent! The virtual absence of hair that is its distinctive feature is due to a genetic mutation. This accounts for the appearance of nude cats at various times throughout the world. This "anomaly" was pointed out in a couple of French Siamese in 1938 and then on an alley cat in Canada in 1966. The spontaneous mutation responsible for this physical particularity is due to a recessive gene. The presence of these nude cats aroused no interest on the North American continent; it was in Europe—in the Netherlands and France—that selections led to the breed as we know it. To build up the pedigree, breeders used the Devon Rex in particular, certain features of which remain, including the large ears or the angular shape of the head. Although subsequently imported back to the United States, the Sphynx remains very scarce. Only unions between Sphynxes are authorized today.

Despite its virtual nudity, this cat does not appear frail and is, on the contrary, very muscular. Lack of hair does not mean lack of pigment, and the standard recognizes all colors. The head is an angular, slightly triangular wedge and is surprising with its huge, well-spaced eyes. Kittens are born with very wrinkled skin and a slight coat on the back that disappears with age.

Extroverted and cheerful, Sphynxes are playful, independent cats. With their all-embracing curiosity, they are sociable and affectionate, but not aggressive. Relatively possessive with their masters, they love being the center of attention and being made a fuss of.

The hairless skin makes them sensitive to cold, as well as to heat and humidity. They are therefore better suited to apartment living. In winter, food portions should be increased to give them extra warmth. In summer, exposure to the sun is dangerous for their skin, and if they have to stay outdoors, they need sunscreen protection.

Unlike other cats, Sphynxes perspire like humans through the skin, thus making regular cleansing necessary. The ears should also be cleaned regularly with a suitable veterinary product.

Reproduction is complicated for this cat, given the fact that females are on heat for a limited period only, and the high neonatal mortality rate makes breeding difficult.

Sphynx, black

Thai, seal point

THAI

Other name: Thai Siamese
Country of origin: Thailand
Ancestors: as for Siamese
Coat: short, dense, lying close to the body, soft to the touch
Colors: all the colors in the colorpoint category

The Thai corresponds to the original variety of Siamese that breeders have attempted to reproduce through selective outcrossings. A breed in its own right since 2002, the Thai standard is quite different from that of the Siamese, established in January 2004. The head is markedly rounder, with a visible break, and the body is more robust. Furthermore, this cat's weight is surprising for its size. The eyes are systematically bright blue, and the coat has a "colorpoint" pattern, characterized by a light ground and darker points in well-defined areas, ensuring a stark contrast. Like the Siamese, the Thai is born white, with the points becoming colored only progressively and taking on their definitive hue between the age of twelve and fifteen months.

The Thai is a very recent creation. This breed arose from selective efforts by breeders seeking to return to the archetypal Siamese, as selections had led away from this by producing rangy and extremely distinctive-looking cats. It thus shares a common history with the Siamese, and its ancestors are said to have been the guardians of the royal treasures of the temples of Siam.

Through selective unions breeders have therefore produced a cat that has a similar colorpoint pattern but is rounder, heavier, and markedly less Oriental in features than the modern Siamese. It is impossible today to confuse it with the Siamese. Indeed, the Thai's morphology is quite distinct, with a fairly short, triangular head; well-filled cheeks; a slight break visible in profile; and a highly muscular, semi-foreign body type that is surprisingly heavy given the cat's build. Very graceful, the Thai is an athletic cat. Only unions between Thais are authorized today, and an appearance too close to that of the Siamese (such as a straight profile or almond-shaped eyes) is penalized in cat shows.

More rustic than today's Siamese and more "natural" in appearance, the Thai has won the public over, and there are more and more amateurs of this old-time Siamese, even if the number of Thais remains limited.

Thais are affectionate and appealing cats that often seek their masters' attention, to whom they are staunchly loyal. They need to be fully involved in family life and do not take well to being alone.

Less vocal than the Siamese, Thais are similarly possessive. Sensitive and emotional, they require care and attention to be happy in a household. Sociable toward other animals, they appear more distant with unfamiliar faces.

Playful and mischievous, they are also highly intelligent and are quick to understand what is expected of them. Their maintenance is easy and consists only of a weekly brushing.

Thai, seal point

TONKINESE

Other names: Golden Siamese, Chocolate Siamese, Tonkanese
Country of origin: United States
Ancestors: Siamese, Burmese
Coat: short, dense, lying close to the body, very silky, glossy, particularly soft to the touch
Colors: typical Siamese markings on a darker ground color, which corresponds to the Burmese coloring though toned down slightly. Three possible patterns: sepia, point, or mink (midway between the two), and can come in blue, chocolate, lilac, red, cream.

Tonkinese, lilac mink

The Tonkinese brings together characteristics that were found in Siamese and Burmese breeds in the 1930s. The Siamese were less Oriental-looking, and the Burmese less rounded. The colorpoint and sepia genes of these two breeds are co-dominant and are therefore both present, thus giving rise to an intermediate shade called mink (which also refers to the fur's characteristic appearance). Unions between Tonkinese subsequently led to the colorpoint and sepia varieties.

The definitive color is not established until around the age of eighteen months, and it tends to darken as the cat gets older. Likewise, it takes some time before the eyes reach their definitive shade. There is a semi-longhaired variety of Tonkinese known as "Tibetan."

The first Tonkinese appeared in the 1930s in the United States, the result of outcrossings between Siamese and Burmese. The breed had difficulty in becoming established as breeders initially lost interest in it before developing it in the 1950s. Unions were soon extended to Tonkinese obtained by crossing Siamese with Burmese, and these alliances made it possible to obtain new colors, notably by restoring the Siamese's colorpoint pattern and the Burmese's sepia pattern. Resurgences of Siamese- or Burmese-type

Tonkinese, lilac mink

kittens remain frequent today in Tonkinese litters. In addition, unions between Siamese and Burmese are still authorized.

The breed was recognized in the late 1970s. Well-developed in the United States, it has had a hard time becoming established in Europe and is still not officially recognized by all cat federations.

Medium in size, the Tonkinese is an elegant cat that is neither cobby nor Oriental in features. The eyes are blue-green or aquamarine in color. The texture of the coat is reminiscent of mink and is particularly soft and pleasant to the touch.

Lively and active, Tonkineses are dynamic cats, ever ready to play or to explore a new territory. They are athletic and appreciate enough space to allow them to ferret about outside. Tonkineses are not couch potatoes and need activity.

Their dynamic nature does not make them any less loving or affectionate, and they are highly attached to their masters, though not exclusive in their relations like their Siamese relative. Yet they detest being alone and do require attention. They are only happy if fully involved in family life. Gentle and sensitive, they get on well with other cats and other animals if raised alongside them.

The short hair is very easy to maintain and requires only weekly brushing.

Turkish Van, auburn and white

TURKISH VAN

Other names: Lake Van
Country of origin: Turkey
Coat: semi-longhaired, fine, soft, silky with the minimum possible woolly undercoat. In summer, the fur is almost short. In winter, it can be considerably fuller.
Colors: white with a distinctive motif called the "Van pattern." Ideally, only the base of the ears, the head, and the tail are colored red or cream.

The Turkish Van is a sturdy cat, with a body that is long, strong, and solidly built. The coat is white with a "Van pattern," which refers to colored markings on the head and tail. On the head, only the base of the ears is symmetrically colored, with the two sides separated by a white blaze. Another red or cream mark may run from the rump to the tip of the tail. Some disparities are tolerated (e.g., a white tail tip or fewer than three markings on the body). All white coloring is also possible, in which case the cat is called "Van Kedisi."

The Turkish Van, in all likelihood related to the Turkish Angora, developed in the region of Lake Van in Turkey. This therefore "natural" breed is very old, yet it only aroused breeders' interest in the mid-1950s when a British breeder decided to import some to start rearing in Europe. A further fifteen years went by before the pedigree was recognized. It then began to be exported to other countries, throughout Europe and to the United States. The Turkish Van remains very rare outside of its country of origin and, being somewhat overshadowed by the Turkish Angora, is struggling to become established.

Stockier than the Angora, the Turkish Van is a cat of large build. The head is long, wider in males than in females, and the large, expressive eyes are blue or gold in color; odd eyes are acceptable and green tolerated. The fur varies greatly according to season. Almost short in summer, it is longer and denser in winter, forming a ruff and britches. The fur may be very plush in older males. Only unions within the breed are accepted.

As a legacy of the region of its origins, the Turkish Van is highly robust and has developed a taste that is quite atypical among cat species: it adores water and swims to perfection!

Selection has mellowed its character; though still rustic, Turkish Vans are now affectionate and sociable. They are endowed with strong characters and have an independent streak. This does not prevent them from being highly attached to their masters and even from being quite possessive at times.

Like all cats of large build, they are fairly late in maturing (not before the age of three). Their past does not predispose them to apartment living, and they prefer to have a garden where they can use their hunting talents. The presence of a pool is a plus that will be much appreciated.

Outside of the often-spectacular spring molting period, the fur is not difficult to maintain and a weekly brushing is sufficient.

Turkish Van, white

ALLEY CAT

Other name: house cat
Ancestors: domesticated Egyptian cats
Coat: all kinds
Colors: all

The alley cat does not belong to any specific breed, as it does not fit any pedigree. The breed is widespread but of no monetary value; thus, they are often unfairly considered. Yet, like their pedigreed peers, they deserve respect, care, and attention.

These very natural cats have managed to win over an audience who appreciate their rustic simplicity, their resourcefulness, and their ingenuity. Often known as "European"—wrongly so, as this is an actual breed— the alley cat indisputably tops the charts for originality as, by definition, all morphologies and characters are possible!

Directly descended from the domesticated wildcat around 2600 B.C.E. in Egypt, the alley cat is a free spirit par excellence. It has forged its own character and has learned to adapt to survive.

Having never been subject to selection procedures, the alley cat has remained very free, both physically and in terms of personality. Broadly speaking, it is unpredictable and with it anything is possible. We know for sure that its background has given rise to a cat that is rustic, resourceful, and smart. An alley cat can find a way out of any situation and demonstrates an ingenuity that is at times remarkable. Amusing and funny, they are tough cookies who know how to enchant their masters with their findings and their whimsical characters. Some alley cats are calm and introverted, while others are more assertive and very reckless. All share an innate taste for hunting, but their

Above: alley cat, brown tabby
Facing page: alley cat, tabby and white

abilities often vary according to their lifestyle—whether they have an outdoor existence or are housecats. Alley cats are also esteemed by their owners in farms or country houses for their mousing prowess.

Alley cats, whose ancestors learned to adapt to survive in the wild, are malleable cats whose behavior is shaped by the environment in which they live. Far from being a "sub-species," they make ideal companions and are well loved for their rustic simplicity and originality, as no two are alike. In every country throughout the world, they prevail over their pedigreed peers, whose numbers remain very much in the minority in comparison. Their distribution network is very disparate and includes family, friends, and animal shelters. In a household, the alley cat is often an institution.

We may consider that alley cats have even earned their pedigree as they are admitted to cat shows and compete in the "housecat" category, which is open to felines of all backgrounds. It is therefore hard to define an alley cat, which on principle answers to no standard, either in terms of physique or behavior. And it is most probably for this reason that we love our alley cats!

Brushing regularity depends on type of coat.

Above: alley cat, black and white
Facing page: alley cat, tricolor

Acknowledgments

Michel Viard would like to extend his grateful thanks to the owners and breeders who entrusted their finest cats to his lens:

Olga Antini
Chatterie Bolshoycat

Corinne and Jean-François Audoin
Peyrat Cattery
Web site: elevagedepeyrat.free.fr

Bernard Baigneaux
Highland Cattery
Tel.: +33 (0)3 44 69 27 11

Christiane and Bernard Boucher
Fort de la Bosse Marnière Cattery
Web site: www.labossemarniere.com

Catherine Cadic
Somalis et Abyssins de Cadicha
Web site: somaliabyssin.free.fr

Adrienne and Jean-Sylvain Chaussard

Bernard and Ghislaine Clerget
Oracle de l'Orient Cattery
Tel.: +33 (0)6 60 07 71 59
Web site: www.chatterie-oracle-de-lorient.com

Pascal Deve
La Cyriellette Cattery

Valérie Dubois-Pobé
Honey Paw Cattery
Tel.: +33 (0)6 70 30 18 13
Web site: www.honeypaw.com

Kévin Duffroy
Royaume de Morgane Cattery

Monique and Gérard Dumont
L'Arche Féline
La Tendre Complicité Cattery
Tel.: +33 (0)2 35 23 10 93
Web site:
perso.orange.fr/la.tendre.complicite

Véronique and Raymond Goy

Christine Job
Dieu Thôt Cattery
Tel.: +33 (0)6 13 50 46 87
Web site: www.chatteriedieuthot.com

Martine Leclerc
Rousseuil Cattery

Annie Leprêtre
Valmont Halatta Cattery
Tel.: +33 (0)6 71 78 21 59
Web site: du-valmont-halatta.com

Catherine Le Trionnaire
Singapuras Partner's Club
Web site: www.singapura.fr

Véronique Liévin
Les Rêves d'Avalon Cattery

Regina Martino
Élevage Regina Rex

Patrick Mayere
Cœur Sauvage Cattery
Web site: www.coeursauvage.net

Suzanne Piqué
Val aux Biches Cattery
Tel.: +33 (0)1 39 57 54 51

Pascal Pobé
Cristalline Blue Cattery
Tel.: +33 (0)6 70 30 18 13

Sophie Rigaud
Cœur de Van Cattery
Web site: web.mac.com/coeurdevan

Elena Suarez-Thouvenin
Sulena de Tengri'Nor Cattery
Tel.: +33 (0)3 44 08 48 95
Web site: desulenadetengrinor.site.voila.fr

France Vandenabeele
Nefertiti Cattery
Tel.: +33 (0)1 39 94 45 43
Web site: www.nefertiti-sphynx.com

Thanks also go to Gisèle Pichard and Pascal Pobé for their assistance, to Monique and Gérard Dumont of L'Arche Féline for their patience and kindness, and to La Boutique Féline for the loan of accessories (www.boutique-feline.fr).

Facing page: Bengal, brown spotted tabby

Photographic credits

All photos are from Agence Horizon Features (www.horizonfeatures.com) and are by Michel Viard.

Translated from the French by Susan Schneider
Design: Nadège Deschildre/Studio Horizon
Copyediting: Karen Heil
Typesetting: Gravemaker+Scott, Edinburgh
Proofreading: Kate van den Boogert

Distributed in North America by Rizzoli International Publications, Inc.

Originally published in French as *Chats*
© Flammarion S.A., Paris, 2007

English-language edition
© Flammarion S.A., Paris, 2008

87, quai Panhard et Levassor
75647 Paris Cedex 13

www.editions.flammarion.com

08 09 10 3 2 1

ISBN-13: 9782080300669

Dépôt légal: 09/2008

Printed in Malaysia by Tien Wah Press